salmonpoetry
Publishing Irish & International
Poetry Since 1981

the arts council
an chomhairle ealaíon

funding
literature
artscouncil.ie

Reckonings

PATRICK MORAN

Acknowledgments are due to the editors of the following where many of these poems, or versions of them, have appeared: *Ambit, Cork Literary Review, Crannóg, Cyphers, Poetry Ireland Review, Southword, Sunday Miscellany* (RTE Radio One), *The Stony Thursday Book, The Warwick Review* and *Wildeside*.

This collection is published in 2019 by
Salmon Poetry, Cliffs of Moher, County Clare, Ireland
www.salmonpoetry.com e: info@salmonpoetry.com
Copyright © Patrick Moran, 2019
ISBN 978-1-912561-69-8

Cover & Title Page Image: *Jessie Lendennie*
Cover Design & Typesetting: *Siobhán Hutson*
Printed in Ireland by Sprint Print

*Salmon Poetry gratefully acknowledges the support of
The Arts Council / An Chomhairle Ealaíon*

for all my care

Contents

Behind these lines,
a lost acolyte,
bent on salvaging…

SWOOP

I was trundling my red train along the yard.
Stop wobbling, I prayed. *Don't topple over!*
When – flashingly, out of nowhere – a bird

came darting through the shed's open doorway,
and disappeared into the dusty blackness.
I begged my father to take me to the nest.

As we stepped into the dark, the swallow
flew over us, so close I could hear its swish.
When he lifted me up on his shoulders,

I couldn't see into the cup; but let
my fingers touch its smoothed lip, and pat
the feathers which lined the tiny, warm bowl...

For days after, I moped about, longing
to retrieve that hit-and-miss experience:
the bare, uneven yard; the air windless,

humid; my father somewhere, hovering.
Then suddenly the swallow there, calling
swit-swit-swit; as suddenly rising, risen

beyond my straining sight, and out of reach.

TRACES

I would spend hours there observing
birds at the bird-table squabbling
    over the crumbs I set.

One day, a blundering pigeon
crashed into a window: the dust
    and oil from its feathers

leaving an imprint on the pane.
Didn't the Holy Spirit descend,
    miraculous as that?

For weeks after, I'd watch the faint
outline become clearer – vivid –
    as the sun was setting.

Until, gradually, the wind
and rain wore every trace away...
    That collision, the wobbling

back on course; and the catechism's
words I just learned by rote gleaming
    on the bird-ghosted glass.

SNAPSHOTS

Sometimes, before entering,
I, their first-born, would pause

on the threshold until
his rumbling thunder,

her brittle lightning flashes
would subside. I, cowering

there: torn, lost for words.

*

You and your figaries,
my father is spluttering.

Imagine saying Mass
at our kitchen table —

and dragging your brothers in
as altar servers!..

Bad enough to have one son
away with the fairies.

*

Sweeping the yard, I find,
beneath the mud and dung,

these cobbles set
like a clutch of eggs.

*

In the river flowing
through our pasture, I magic

the twig I float
into a boat I'm rowing

down the Amazon
or the Orinoco...

PLUMS

My mother is leading me by the hand –
I, a dreamy boy still absorbed
in fairy tales, in whisperings
about raths and ghostly ruins –
down a lane marked by ruts and hooves;
past the stubbles, the looming stooks,
down to the orchard's apples, plums.

First, I taste the apples – the Charles Ross,
pale cream beneath the orange-red flush –
then stow them in a shopping bag.
But the plums! I fondle the yellow,
freckled skin; I gorge on them,
my teeth piercing the rough, sweet flesh,
the juice dribbling down my chin...

And, afterwards, tiptoeing back
in thickening dusk – feeling the weight
of the bulging bag; the fruit coming
bitterly back up my throat –
I clutch her hand more tightly now...
What's lurking in the creeping fog?
Is that stook of barley stirring?

FODDERING

We'd set out, my father and I,
with the pony and cart, to tend
    the cattle wintering

in an outlying field: their breath
steaming in the chill, as the load
    was spread on the hard ground.

Every fork of hay he pitched
I'd hollow to nest the turnips in,
    until the cart was bare…

Then, turning homewards, yearning still
to sense an opening that would spring
    Daddy from my tongue.

But never a softening word or touch,
down that narrow, winding road.
    Only dog-barks, far off;

a tractor chugging towards Clonboo;
and my father sinking deeper
    in the clip-clop rhythm.

TALKING IN MY SLEEP

Where do they come from, these wellings
and unravellings which jolt me awake;

which are beyond my family's
fretting or fathoming;

which stop abruptly in mid-air,
yet keep echoing there?

LIVES OF THE SAINTS

In her sober black outfit
and a lovely
crocus-yellow blouse,

my aunt would search her bag
for the slim booklet. *Look:
another saint for you!*

*

When Thuringia
was ravaged by plague
and famine, Elizabeth

of Hungary renounced
wealth: distributing alms,
building an hospital.

Once, secretly taking
bread to the stricken,
she was challenged;

but when they opened
her bulging pouch, they found
the loaves transformed to roses.

*

Looking out on the vast plain
of Fanjeaux, Dominic
saw a star descend

over the church at Prouille:
God's sign, as he believed,
to start his life's work there.

Fearlessly confronting
the Albigenses;
his arguments cutting

like flaming scourges
so that the heretics
could only foam in rage.

*

On snow-white nights, I'd ponder
Catherine of Siena's
penitential fasting,

her jubilation
at shearing her long hair.
In the Basilica

di San Domenico,
her entombed head
incorruptible.

*

Turning the pages,
I could see Matt Talbot
on his bare plank bed;

could see the chains and cords
unwinding from his flesh
after death: the zeal

of self-denial
still visible
in the reddened indentations.

*

I'd wonder if prayer
and abstinence

could earn for me even
a little miracle…

To be free of nightmares
pouncing on my sleep.

To be spring-heeled
in leaping for the ball.

To unfurrow my father's
brow, thaw out his tongue.

CAGED BIRDS AT MIGRATION TIME

In the deepening nights,
they would come back to me,

those caged birds I'd read about
in my big bird book: pining

for flight and breeding...
zugunruhe.

I could feel them behind the bars,
hopping, whirring, flapping:

helplessly rehearsing
take-offs from their perches;

wings forever straining
across make-believing skies.

CAUGHT

Reading a crime thriller,
I trail the PI, David Flame,
down the mean streets of Singapore:

mulling over every clue;
listening to lives unravel;
rushing into cul-de-sacs.

Turning each beguiling page,
I wait, credulous, for the last
pieces to fit in. Only to fall

through the trapdoor springing open:
that affable old man exposed
as a traitor, a double agent.

SCHOLARSHIP BOY

Winning my way to boarding school
struck me like a bolt from the blue:
Was this where dreaminess and a love
    of words were leading me?

To leave all I'd known for Latin,
Greek, a uniform? To be cast
in neighbours' eyes as a wonder...*strange?*
    Would I become a priest?...

Already, handshakes, good wishes –
'Twill be the making of you yet! –
tangling with jibes behind my back:
    Sissy!..Teacher's pet!

LEAVING MY AUNT'S HOUSE: AUGUST 1963

All that had been between us —
those slim *Lives of the Saints*
she'd bequeath to me;

the Saint Patrick's Day badges,
into which she stitched
sprigs of real shamrock,

pinned on my lapel;
our ears tuned to the radio:
hurling matches, awesome feats —

unspoken now; but implicit
in this sprinkling
of holy water

to wish me well
as I started boarding school:
her parting words in my ears —

You're leaving all this behind! —
as I cycled homewards
along the winding road.

Past that skeletal house;
past a cart bearing
a rickety load of straw.

Then the fog creeping
under hedges, across
aftergrass and stubbles.

And the road darkening
as I freewheeled, open-
mouthed, down the hill,

hoping to avoid
the potholes beyond
my flashlamp's wavering arc!

THE DEAN OF DISCIPLINE ADDRESSES US

The Junior Dean of Discipline (Joe Stal)
addressed us that first morning. He's wrinkled, bald:
a single strand of hair oiled to his skull.

Formation, lasting values!... Here, my dear boys,
we aim to mould you into strong Christians –
thick pebble glasses glinting, his eyes raised –

boys who tell the truth, who give good example,
frequent the sacraments: boys fit, indeed,
to join our seminary!..But, above all,

never yield (his Adam's apple rubbing
against the Roman collar) *to impure thoughts.*
His points made with head-nods, finger-jabbing...

Next time, we will discuss how courtesy
and etiquette can make us godlier.
Come to our aid, O Lord. Now, let us pray.

ALMA MATER

Jack Knack explaining
the college motto,
Hiems transiit

(Winter has passed):
how the repealing
of the Penal Laws

led to the opening
of St. Kieran's College,
school and seminary.

*

I'd trudge down deserted
corridors, my feet wheezing
on the polished lino;

the walls lined with photos
of ordination groups:
serene, invulnerable.

From somewhere, piano
notes: bursting in my heart,
my vision blurring…

*

And no escaping.
From the shadows, I'd observe
clique after clique

going around the walks.
Emerging into view,
bantering and laughing;

then turning the corner,
their cosy chat receding
beyond my straining ears.

*

Everything closing in.
My days dragging
like a ball and chain.

THE GLASS HALL

A frosty winter's evening:
First Years are jostling each other
    off the crowded forms.

On the window ledges, lads play
push penny: their combs sweeping coins
    through the gouged-out markings.

But table tennis lures me more.
I could watch forever Dollard's
    graceful backhand smashes,

his looping forehands overcoming
Farrell's cagey spins, Kennedy's
    monotonous ping-pong.

*

Hair modish as a Rolling Stone's,
Dodger is prowling. I recoil, dreading
    sneers, his squeezing fingers.

But, trying to twist Walsh's arm,
he's elbowed back; and told: *Feck off,*
    ya dirty wanker.

I'm learning that the bad language
Mam warned me against is better
    shielding, more effective

than my fine words, my meek, priestly
eyes when they chant *Moron, Moron!*
    with mischievous disdain.

*

Groups pass by; low talk, receptive
ears. Tongues rise to matches, explode
          in smutty jokes: *Diddies!*

I'm growing *inconspicuous*:
fearing what lurks in voices, what
          is said behind my back.

Sometimes, I flee to the toilets,
letting words burrow deep: *Bereft.*
          Trauma. Panacea.

Prefects swish past in long soutanes.
Dollard is lording it! Someone
          stoops for a fallen coin.

I look across the lawn, thinking
of the skivvies: those mute voices;
          that deferential bearing.

And imagine their bleak lodgings
lit up, their radios blaring
          out of open windows.

THE THIRTY YEARS' WAR

Nailer, brisk as ever:
Open chapter eight,
The Thirty Years' War.

Causes? Religious conflicts.
Recurring power struggles...
Underline, memorise!

And then catching me doodling,
taking off from text books,
the columned blackboard, he'd swoop:

What do you think, Moran?
The class would giggle. *Are you*
away again in dreamland?

*

Beyond the orderly
accounts, beyond my homework,
I'd keep imagining

the armies advancing
through forests, between fields
of ripening corn.

Doors broken down, smoking
ruins, women screaming,
blood flowing down the streets.

Diseases invading
ravaged flesh; bubonic
plague, typhus, dysentery.

The stunted obsequies,
hurried burials, hearts
lined with graveyard crosses.

*

Sometimes, when I'd recite
to myself the names
as if in litany

Brandenburg Bohemia
Tilly Maximilian
Brietenfeld Barwalde

the images of war
would yield to syllabic
pulse and rhythm

Bremen Stiria
Saxony Nordlingen
Ratisbon Rocroi

hatching, lifting off my tongue.

NICKNAMES

Paul E. Butler (whose voice squeaked; who read books,
never togged out for games) would be set upon.
Coming from the chapel, queuing for meals,
they'd taunt him: *Polly, put the kettle on!*

One day in Latin class when Knack was teaching
Virgil, spouting about Palinurus,
Doyle smirking – had it come after musing,
or in a flash? – whispered: *Pollynudus!*

*

No one laid a hand on Canice.
But then, contagious as a rash,
the whispers spread, ear to ear. Until
it burst into the open: BOSH!

An acronym, some bright spark said:
the nickname haunting like a curse.
What's that? they'd ask, to rouse the chant.
Bodily Odoured Smelly Horse!

So no escape. Around corners,
in corridors, huddles, giggles.
It would be lurking in a cough;
or pounce from toilet cubicles.

And none of us reached out to him,
a curly-haired boy slipping away
through flood plains, test tubes, dative verbs;
The Tempest, metrics, piety…

STIRRINGS

Now that the dorm is dark,
now that the vigilant
prefect's steps are still,

I am ready to indulge
in these imaginings:
fugitive, risky...

I'm roasting, Noreen says,
as she casts off her clothes.
Gorgeous, irresistible...

(Dear God, I am sorry;
and I firmly resolve
never to sin again.)

But for abusing
my body, the temple
of the Holy Spirit:

how could I confess it?
And what if God – or Stal –
should find out what I've done;

should see the stiffened patch
on my pyjamas' crotch,
the sheet's snot-coloured stain?

MR. B'S ENGLISH CLASS

Our boisterous class calming
as Mr. B enters,
his zeal swaying

even the indifferent.
"Poetry, boys! Open
Tennyson's *Lotos-Eaters*."

Reciting it, he lounges
to suggest the ease
of the sailors in repose;

or, with groans and furrowed brow,
he mimics their rowing
through a storm.

"Revel in the sounds:
Music that gentlier
on the spirit lies...

Let words trip off your tongue:
The surge was seething free —
can ye hear the tumult?

Now, boys: imagine
those crisping ripples,
unfading amaranth.

Visualise
yourselves reclining
on beds of asphodel!"

STRAY

That evening in study,
during that final May,
what was it prompted
my biro to stray

off the homework track
to a tempting blank sheet:
Chance, some vague destiny?
Or just to seek respite

from tedious Gaelic texts;
chemical formulae;
baffling calculations;
ancient Roman history?

But, scribbling there, how could I know
where it would take me?
That this dark, furtive burrowing
would shake me, make me?

Jotting my thoughts, I felt
like a calf released to grass:
the rhythm new and strange,
the word-flow mysterious…

I feel like Catherine
at the window beating:
Let me in – let me in!…

These unresting nights,
I imagine my father's fields

as a kind of paradise.
Spring shoots pushing up.

Corn stooks bulking in stubbles.
Mangolds tinged with orange…

I dream I'm no longer
on the outside looking in;

but playing a hurling match,
with the outcome finely poised,

and only minutes left:
the sliotar bobbing towards me

to strike past the keeper
for the winning,

reverberating score!

MY LAST ORDINATION SUNDAY

I knelt for the blessing
of the newly ordained priests;

I bowed to sanctifying hands,
to lips charged with healing;

responding *Amen, Amen…*
The vestigial altar boy

in me flickering, still waiting
for the loaves and fishes

to multiply, for the water
to shimmer into wine.

LEAVINGS

Last weeks, final exams looming…
But we'd relax with Father Gus:
his handouts on faith and morals
later flying as paper arrows.

He'd tell us about reformed Saul,
and Dominic braving the Cathars;
or doomed young Guy de Fontgalland,
delirious as heaven neared…

But our hearts were breaking cover,
pulsing with callow lust-in-love.
I understood; yet felt the pang
of all that was slipping through the sieve.

III

NEW YEAR'S EVE: 1975

Only this compulsive questing
down roads that narrow to dead ends.

Only rumblings, staccato beats.
Fag-ash. Leftovers. One-night stands.

Only these Hamletic musings
on blotted sheets, unfilling hands.

SNOW

The cortege crawling through
snowy streets: Tim Boyle's corpse
being hearsed to church.

Barely 40, they said.
What happened? That failed romance?
A history coming back

to haunt him? We recalled
his drunken babble
as he'd fill petrol:

the nozzle shaking,
the erratic flow, acrid
drizzling spillage…

*

After, in the pub, dodging
funeral musings, we watched
the settling Guinness darken;

waited our turn at pool.
Chalking, cueing, potting
the balls: my faith wavering

as a would-be winning black
stalled on the pocket's lip.
I drifted to the slot machine,

hoping the fruity symbols
stiffen in a row,
disgorge a glut of coins.

*

Unable to sleep,
I was drawn out of doors,
beckoned on and on

across an expanse
as smooth, as unblemished
as an altar cloth.

How had I come to this?
Teetering on the roll
of a ball, spinning reels.

And every trace of snow
in me fraying away,
weathering to slush?

REMEDIAL

Is this my true vocation?
To mould and quicken,

keep faith with these students:
that here, amid stalling

biros, faulty syntax,
ingrained misspellings,

the rumblings at the back,
words might yet be beacons,

and fledgling wings somehow
wobble into flying?

JUVENILIA

A heart appeasing
its haunted strains:
rebukes and fissures

rooted in childhood;
barbs arrowing home
on a school corridor...

A spirit still charged
with awe at church bells,
delicate hedges.

A voice, muffled
with echoes, shaping
to be delivered.

A pen venturing
across blank sheets, greeting
word-fits with *eureka!*

NIGHTCLUBBING

The lights dimming,
the music's rhythm slowing
for the final set...

Again, I reach out
to the girls, their perfumed
aura and nyloned thighs:

Will you dance please?
They appraise my dithering;
my dark, unsettling eyes.

Then turn away: as if
divining, in my depths,
slippage, quicksand.

POKER SESSIONS

Our cigarette smoke rising
like slowly drifting incense,

we'd watch the shuffling and dealing:
keeping faith with meagre hands,

hoping to be composed
in house or blue or run...

Afterwards, I'd brood
on my diffidence and wavering:

Why, with three queens,
did I yield to bluffing?

Or, holding aces,
not raise the betting?..

In the random scatterings,
in every might-have-been

intimations of grace,
a glimmer of epiphany.

IN THE SMALL HOURS

Tonight, in the throes
of nightmare – boarding school
bullies pounding the door

I am quaking behind:
Moron, Moron! – I'm jolted
out of slumber…

Groping towards the toilet,
I'm quivery, open
to ghostly intimations…

of vigil light, sanctuary?
But nothing answering
only a bird's shrilling,

some cow in a shed
or a pasture
forlornly lowing.

LAST CLASS

After another day of planting
words and opening books, of coaxing
pens across blank pages, I watch

my students leave, their tongues loosened
by other gods: some pop star's rousing
lyrics, a Man United goal...

Then check desks: erasing graffiti,
arrowed hearts; tending abandoned
books like birds caught in an oil-slick.

WRITERS' GROUP: 1982

Jean hatching an epic
set in Gorey, the heroine
to be named Satana.

Paul, an earnest loner,
clutching a dog-eared
copy of Lowell's poems.

Cathy content to laud
sunsets and daffodils
in swaddling, hackneyed rhymes...

A fraught, tiptoeing air.
Soulful outpourings submitted
to forked appraising tongues.

And I there – flashing, rumbling –
waiting to be shaken
into cloudbursts, teeming rain.

*

A workshop questionnaire:
Reflections on your writing?

*Behind my lines, a lost
acolyte bent on salvaging...*

*When I've made a poem,
this strange unease – as if*

*whatever I ached to quell
still lurked beyond my grasp.*

*

Does it atone somewhat,
divining a phrase like

via dolorosa,
for mistaken turnings;

engine failings; skids;
the potholes I keep jolting through?

*

To be wide-eyed, open
as I cultivate my lines…

To capture hushed arenas
where hearts are waiting

for a shot that curls beyond
the goalie's stretching hand.

To register the suspense
in a back-room's smoky haze

as cards are shuffled, scattered.
To hold a nightclub's ferment,

to find its tingling rhythms.
Letting words and spirit press…

into plenitude
or emptiness?

*

I'm a pipe fit to burst:
my words ready

to redress grievances,
absolve the past...

Against the old dismay –
Mop it up! Call a plumber! –

I'd secretly exult
in the gush and spillage.

*

Submissions, offerings.
Another clutch of poems,

reaching for a lifeline
in journals, magazines,

comes slinking back,
rejection slip attached.

WILD OATS

A nightclub's beckoning
lights, its exalting beats:
stirrings of *Adoro*...

Another woman.
Gropings, opening lips;
her shimmering snow.

Another morning.
Stale perfume. Echoes: jagged
talk, receding heels.

DART

Hearing that July night,
you'd been found in some outhouse,
dead by your own hand,

I thought of your crumpled
report sheet: *Disruptive.*
No homework. Late – again.

And how, when challenged,
you'd just mutely shrug,
then slouch away…

As you'd keep slouching back,
fretting me with questions:
Was my teaching freeing

voices? Or tightening nets?
And, sometimes, in restive
classes, I'd half-expect

a paper plane – like those
you'd lovingly adorn
and launch from your back desk –

to dart through the air:
wobbling late in flight,
nosediving at my feet.

REMAINS

After years of chasing losses,
of wayward cards and also-rans;

years of nightclub dreams wilting
in rebuffs, a perfume whiff,

you walked, one night, down the railway,
smack into a coming train.

They salvaged what they could of you;
they went through the old ceremonies,

lowered the coffin in the grave.
But your remains were everywhere...

Your severed head, your blood-streaked hair
cropping up in nightmares.

Your reluctant smile fluttering
at discos, at weddings.

Your disembodied bones
at every burial.

AFTERINGS

When they told me that BOSH
was found, dead for days,

in some seedy bedsit,
his name echoed back the years

like a leper's bell.
I heard too late…

But what would I have done?
Try to word my way through?

As if, failing all,
line and rhythm

could redeem a history,
or cushion his fall?

MAYDAY: 1984

Drinks filling, emptied.
Huddlings. Low talk, guffaws.

At cards, I'm mired in bets
and bluffing; aces, duds…

Flapping towards another
closing time, am I

taking off? Or merely
setting in my ruts?

DROPOUT

The exercises
I'd set to encourage
self-expression —

essays; diary-keeping;
exploring a poem —
meant nothing to him.

Even then, he'd become
as articulate
as he would ever be:

his history
(its wounds, its rumblings;
its cravings and regrets)

stitched into his voice,
his disposition: the gruff
responses; the shrugging;

the evasive eyes;
his pen aggressively
doodling on copies...

Still, when he'd gone,
he hovered over my teaching
like a question mark.

He who spurned moulding,
who kept slipping from my grasp,
what had schooling given him?

Dead texts, red biro scrawls?
Rebukes like shutting doors?
And sometimes, too, I'd muse

on his distinctive bearing:
Would it make or break him?
Would he outgrow the labels —

misfit, loner, troublemaker —
I had pinned on him?
Or would those tags define him,

harden into badges?

MAKINGS

I, their first-born, visiting:
still tangled in their strains,
my voice costive, staccato…

My mother blind, wheelchair-bound.
Her face puffed, her stomach queasy
from the regimen of pills.

My father gruffly attentive:
his words tiptoeing through
landmines set… how long ago?

*

Now the garden's gone
beyond his tending hands,
he gathers kindling:

poking the hedges
for brittle twigs;
or in the fuel shed,

amid turf slivers
and broken laths,
assembling a pile

of flattened cartons.
In these cast-offs, these worn
fingers fire for winter?

*

She listens to tapes
of her favourite songs, over

and over: *Doonaree,
Teddy O'Neill, Boolavogue…*

Is she trying,
in a ferment

of memory and yearning,
to compose her pains, her frets?

Are her reveries beaconing
her darkened road?

Or shunting her
towards cul-de-sacs?

*

And I turning my restless days —
their fickle epiphanies,
their seepages and might-have-beens —

into jottings, numbered pages:
as if the unrecorded life
were not worth living.

THE GRIP

Sometimes, when I'd be marking
exercises or groping
for a poem, it would all come back...

My father's hands
(huge, calloused) gripping
my pencil-holding fingers,

teaching me to write,
letter after letter,
guiding me between the lines...

Was he charging me
with his restive dreams, or
urging me beyond them?

Were the words we made
pointing towards an open road
or yielding cul-de-sacs?

DIVINING

When I cast for that altar now —
the bread, the wine; the bowed heads; up-
      lifting *Introibo* —

what stirs is not some hoary god;
but words quickening, spilling until
      I'm shaking like a rod.

THE DAY PHILIP LARKIN DIED

That night, in the pub,
amid rituals

of spirit measures, draining glasses;
amid pool balls thudding,

the cards filling or failing;
amid the regulars'

hoary yarns, the gossip
retailed with edgy zest;

amid muffled reveries
and charged expletives;

in the cracks widening between
the said and the unsayable,

I sensed him somehow there,
sounding out the depths:

our costive souls
glimmering in his lines.

IV

BEATS

for Margaret

These fingers which register
word-spurts, which mark the rhythms,

press into your yielding flesh
like harbingers of love…

After all my faring,
a life set for quickenings –

instinctive, mysterious –
across bare sheets towards

consummation, the makings
of trace and signature.

ROOKS NESTING

Beyond this raucous cawing;
beyond the stubborn urge

to be brooding and hatching;
beyond the heartaches, the mishaps —

nest-makings lost in flight;
storms, vindictive guns;

eggs dashed to smithereens —
can you sense fledglings pulsing

into flight, can you hear
the renewed, distinctive squawking?

ANNIVERSARY

It's part of us forever now,
Dubrovnik, our honeymooning there:
after my questing, drifting years,
    you my rest, my guiding star!..

You seeking tan-perfecting sun,
I gravitating to the shade;
you swimming far out, testing limits,
    I content to stroll and read.

But in the balmy evenings,
bridging tongues and fluttery beats,
our words reclaiming hallowed ground:
    in unison, those nights!

And remember that sudden storm:
thundering, flashing, shaking us
like an argument? By dawn,
    it had gone without a trace.

VOICE

Love, after all our years,
who knows my voice like you:

its muffled flurries
at cards or matches;

its unwearied reaching
for the high notes, its teetering;

its tentative *entrées*,
its quivering release?

And who is better
to read my weathers

in its shades and moulding,
its symptomatic wheeze?

SEAM

Until it's become
a way of life, this wording
into the dark and deep,

this straining to raise
uneasy spirits
in reconciling lines…

But am I mining
tongues of fire? Or fruitlessly
hacking ghostly layers?

And is the bucket
that is lowering me
tied to a fraying rope?

SPECTRAL

My nightly checking,
rechecking: eyes darting
backward, backward

to tightened taps; keys
and switches; blinds
already drawn…

But, deep in sleep,
eerie fingers
pick the locks;

memories rip open
my delicate
stitching; and all

I am clinging
to is slipping
from my grip.

WHODUNIT

I press the button, open
another episode
of *Midsomer Murders,*

Poirot or *Sherlock Holmes*:
letting mystery loose
in my innards. I probe

the clues like a detective
manqué: blood stains; semen traces;
histories festering.

I follow the leads and twists
as questions hover
over confessions, alibis.

Sifting through leavings;
casting; brooding;
quickening, closing in…

And all for what? To scratch
old sores? To feel the orgasmic
quiver of *denouement*?

Or a compulsive craving
to retrieve or recreate
what is lost forever:

that child's whoopee; a humming
kitchen; the girl frisking,
moon-eyed, from a disco?

And hold the weave, shimmering,
against the culprit's pouncing,
the weapon's thrust; against

a world collapsing?

RECKONINGS

Another year is closing in.
So much has come to pass...

Yet still these residual
acolyte's exaltings;

still these oozings,
poulticed in rhyme and rhythm.

And still these ripplings
from stones cast long ago.

The toxins seeping deeper.
Churches emptying.

Bruised silences, stifled lives.
Inquesting. Speculating...

Are my poems glutting
upon relics, dregs?

Am I, in striving forward,
just sinking in my tracks?

CLASS REUNION

Back to my *alma mater*,
to ghostly traces

of the Dean of Discipline
plotting our formation!

I stand in The Glass Hall,
remembering those clustered boys

from fifty years ago,
their bonding chat and jokes.

And I there, moony,
diffident; still yearning

to belong. Yet, dreading
their rebuffs, I'd shrink

inward, desperately
trying to cast crutches.

*

Peering into the old classrooms,
I listen for echoes
of my shaping teachers…

The elegiac strain
in Jack Knack's voice
seeping into me

as he glorified battles,
indomitable spirits:
Hannibal, Leonidas;

Marathon and Cannae.
Or, in hushed tones, lamenting
the fall of Athens:

Spring had gone from the year,
and Greece would never
be the same again…

Or Mr. B absorbing us
in Wordsworth's boy
mimicking the owls;

and that stolen boat
setting furtively out
across the waiting lake.

I, listening, spellbound,
as his tongue would quicken
to melodious rhythms:

But she is in her grave, and, oh,
The difference to me!…
Do ye feel his grief?

The murmurous haunt
of flies on summer eves…
Can ye hear the buzzing?

*

How Father Gus would urge us,
fervent acolytes who bore

the offerings and rang the bells,
to keep God in our hearts, on our lips:

The pure waters of baptism
coursing through your insulated pipes!..

So what would he make of me now,
this leaky, rust-prone conduit

trickling away…and no telling
how much has been lost in transit?

*

I look across the lawn
to where the skivvies lodged:

those lads who served at tables,
who tidied, cleaned for us.

I'd worry about them:
Were they (as my classmates

whispered) from broken homes?
Or *illegitimate?*..

But no trace now of their cramped
huts, their crackling radios.

And I'm no nearer knowing
where they came from,

or where they have gone.
From whose hearts do The Beatles

or Rolling Stones issue still?
What hidden pasts

are infiltrating
like dry rot, atrophy?

*

The seminary is closed:
no more spirit-hatching;
no more priests newly fledged...

Imbued with religious zeal,
I once dreamed of joining
those solemn ordinands;

but my aspiration
to priesthood foundered
on my classmates' scathing
tongues...

Yet now recalling
ordination Sundays,
and those black-robed men

taking off for ministry,
I instinctively
begin to name

the local parishes
and foreign dioceses
they were destined for –

Danesfort, Callan, Tullaroan;
Adelaide, Dunkeld,
Wellington, Monterey –

with all the fervour
of a lost vocation;
with all the aching

of an obituarist
arranging the orderly
disposal of remains.

LESSONS

Now my teaching career is done,
I sometimes sense, hovering,
the ghost of Mr. B:

Yes, you were diligent
in expounding, marking;
in preparing for exams.

But were your red biro marks
beacons or smoking wicks?
Did you ever find the words

to entice your students
from their inner attics?
How many shivered on the heath

with Lear, or heard Catherine
at the window beating?
Who took up their pens and walked?

FUNERALS

In these ends, beginnings…
Beyond the buzz of motorways,
    I go down these worn roads,

    these briary, potholed lanes
to another mourning family,
    as if re-entering

    my proper element.
Past ripening meadows, freeranging
    hedges, steadfast gates; through

    villages and townlands:
Gortnahoe, Galmoy, Bawnaughra,
    Killoran, Lisanure…

*

I dip my fingers
in the holy water font,

and make the sign of the cross
out of ghostly habit.

Sympathising
with the bereaved, I laud

resilience and grace;
or seek words to salvage

blighted lives: elegising
the inklings of a gift,

some glimmering might-have-been.
In reminiscing, I reach

for the vestiges
of my fledgling voice;

its burr, its folk expressions:
Liz was a lovely dancer,

she could turn on a sixpence...
Jack would make that fiddle talk...

No one was handier
with a scythe or hoe than Jim...

*

As I follow the hearse
into the cemetery
for another burial,

everything in me aches
to quicken to epiphany,
to revive a life's openings —

a girl radiant
in her First Communion dress;
a lad sweetstroking the ball

beyond the keeper's reaching;
the bells of consecration
hushing, resonating;

hearts fusing in a summer dance;
turning up the random card
that makes a winning hand;

the first stirrings
of a pregnancy;
a tangle of words

and feelings released
in a heady whiskey —
and hold them luminous

against this death, this box
on which the briskly shovelled clay
is now thudding, thudding.

BULBS

i.m. my father

Last night, I dreamt of him again: this man
whose deft touch could rouse a sluggish fire;
whose nimble fingers knew the inner workings

of clocks and watches; but most, the gardener,
so indulgent he'd let stray cabbages
or spuds flourish in a drill of carrots;

who, even when stooped with age, could still wonder:
Where do all the weeds come out of? This man
whose gifts I lacked, whose ways I wouldn't follow...

So there I was, reluctantly standing
upon a patch of neglected ground, hardly
knowing why. And what should I be setting:

Flowers, shrubs? Organic vegetables?
I was just getting down to work – plotting;
marking; turning scraws over with a spade –

when I came on them, snug as landmines: bulbs
he'd planted years before, still waiting there...
Innocent, helpless, strangely eloquent.

IMPROVISINGS

As a child, it engrossed me
how you, father, would improvise
about the farm:

casually yoking pallets
to block a gap, to make
a hut or chicken-run;

hanging a rusty gate
from a tree trunk; or transforming
half-barrels into feeding racks...

And I'm still drawn
to these inspired contrivings
which survive you,

as if somehow our spirits
could find a belated,
exiguous link

in this instinct
to preserve and embellish:
the faded cream bathtub

granted an afterlife
as a drinking trough;
or that old mattress

sealing a hedge's breach,
its springs showing
through the fraying ticking.

EMBRYONIC

The diaries you kept, mother,
like a fenced-off paddock:
did my pen somehow

arise from those?
Each day's allotted
space as confining

as your corset or apron:
only leaving room
for barely recorded

births, marriages and deaths;
church-going; your children's
ailments; the fickle weather…

Dutiful, decorous,
yet rarely expressing
the essential you:

your playful flashes,
that animated eye
for character and foible;

your airy reaches;
your broody, fretted depths.
Did my poems emerge from that?

And was I to be the bull,
snorting at the gate, bursting
through your hedges?

DRESSMAKER

You, who after a day
measuring, cutting, shaping
    coats and suits and dresses

    would itch to crochet
hems, veils, colour-freckled doilies;
    or those elegant hats

    you'd shape in Prussian blue;
tulipy orange-and-red; gauzy
    lilac, flighty yellow...

    Who'd gather our townland –
its lore, its characters, its strays –
    into your glinting eyes,

    what's left now of that gleam,
that nimbleness? Or the words you'd cast,
    deft as lifebelts, dragnets?

DELIVERY

I see you there, cousin Mary,
in your final illness,

straining still, rambling,
reminiscent: a huddle

of *If onlys* flapping against
spinsterish reticence and stays.

Your throwaway shrug,
your oddly giddy laugh

groping for a flourish;
until your words would find

a pure, untrammelled note:
Too late, Paddy, too late!

EXPOSURE

Often now, I brood on them –
whose ardour, whose wounded eyes

might have been my own –
and all that they endured…

For years, betrayals,
violations: children,

women abandoned, abused
in institutions, schools

Magdalen Letterfrack
Goldenbridge Artane…

For years, sealed lips and oozings;
secret burials.

For years, in dark rooms,
images developing;

and words moulding
as memories retrieve

shut-up histories:
dragging into the light

unmasked faces,
uplifting hands.

FAITH OF OUR FATHERS

Testifying, the victim spoke
like one fermenting in recall;
as if this reshaping and telling
    could mitigate or heal.

Back in the Furry Glen, the priest
buggering him on a cream mattress;
then unfolding his purple stole
    to wipe away the mess.

Often, too, when he'd just served Mass:
his sobs blared out by rock'n'roll,
and Bible-waving threats that if
    he blabbed, he'd roast in hell.

Or this, a nightmare still: once, after,
as the priest retrieved his jacket,
a small receptacle for hosts
    slipped, glinting, from the pocket.

PATRICK MORAN was born in Templetuohy, Co. Tipperary, where he still lives with his wife and family. He is a retired post-primary teacher. He has won the Gerald Manley Hopkins Poetry Prize; he has also been a winner at Listowel Writers' Week. In 1990, he was shortlisted for the Hennessy/ Sunday Tribune Poetry Award. His poem, "Bulbs", won Poem for the Ploughing at the 2015 Ploughing Championships. His work is featured in anthologies, including the inaugural *Forward Book of Poetry* (UK), *The Stony Thursday Book*, *Even the Daybreak: 35 Years of Salmon Poetry*, as well as *The Best of Irish Poetry 2007* and *Best Irish Poetry 2010*. He is also represented in *Windharp: Poems of Ireland since 1916*. His work has been broadcast on the RTE radio programme, *Sunday Miscellany*. His previous collections of poetry are: *The Stubble Fields* (Dedalus Press, 2001); *Green* (Salmon Poetry, 2008); and *Bearings* (Salmon Poetry, 2015).

.

salmonpoetry

Cliffs of Moher, County Clare, Ireland

"Like the sea-run Steelhead salmon that thrashes upstream to its spawning ground, then instead of dying, returns to the sea—Salmon Poetry Press brings precious cargo to both Ireland and America in the poetry it publishes, then carries that select work to its readership against incalculable odds."

TESS GALLAGHER

The Salmon Bookshop
& Literary Centre

Ennistymon, County Clare, Ireland